Matthew Clark

SERIAL

KILLERS

UK

A Disturbing Journey in the Most Shocking True Crime Stories in the History of United Kingdom

Table of Contents

Introduction *4*

1. Jack the Ripper *8*

2. Harold Shipman *29*

3. John Christie *46*

4. Graham Young *63*

5. Peter Tobin *85*

6. William Palmer *92*

7. Beverley Allitt *99*

8. Peter Manuel *106*

9. Amelia Dyer *122*

Introduction

The word "serial" means or implies more than one crime, and the term "killer" implies a person who has killed at least three people with a "cooling-off period" in-between each murder. It is estimated that less than 1% of homicides involve serial killers.

How to Spot a Serial Killer?

They usually commit crimes near their home, are not very intelligent, and have problems with authority figures. Real serial killers are not always white, middle-class males. They do not always use a gun, don't jump out of the bushes and start shooting, and don't always have a motive.

It is estimated that serial killers kill an average of 10 people each, with approximately 550 victims in the United States all-time. Some serial killers leave clues at the crime scene; more intelligent serial killers rarely do so. There are no definitive physical characteristics of a serial killer because everyone is unique. Real serial killers tend to be very thorough at concealing evidence. If the crime took place years ago, there might not be any physical evidence left.

Serial killers are very methodical and organized; they plan their crimes in advance and meticulously prepare for them. Some serial killers seek fame, and there is some evidence that these individuals welcome the opportunity to capture their crimes on audiotape or videotape. They sometimes keep souvenirs of their victims such as clothing, jewelry, or body parts (e.g., fingers).

How Do Serial Killers Get Started?

Most serial killers have been abused as children. Serial killers have most likely had a bad relationship with the opposite sex in their teen years, they were bullied as a child, and they seem to be easily manipulated while in prison.

Many serial killers are white males between the ages of 20 and 40. Members of their family abused many; many are loners or social misfits; some had no father figure in their lives, and some were very intelligent. Some serial killers are very athletic, but most are not. Often serial killers have a fascination or an obsession with police work and fire-fighting. Women abused an estimated 75% of serial killers.

What Motivates Serial Killers?

Most serial killers do not fit the stereotype of crazed maniacs who kill for pleasure. Instead, they are usually mature individuals who kill for material gain or want to fulfill their own personal psychological needs. A need for power drives some serial killers, some are driven by an obsession with authority, and some kill for the thrill of it.

Many serial killers are white males between the ages of 20 and 40. Often they have been abused by women in their youth; they can be loners or social misfits. Some were very intelligent. Many had no father figure in their lives; some were very aggressive as children and turned to crime to make up for it; some see violence as a way to relieve frustration.

The motivation of serial killers usually changes over time. Most serial killers start out killing animals and work their way up to humans. Some serial killers do not have trouble controlling their urges; others do. Some kill people and steal from their homes; these are called "organized" killers, while others kill for pleasure and leave behind "impulse" murders. Some murderers are driven by a need for power, some by an obsession with authority, and some kill for the thrill of it; they do not plan or try to conceal evidence. They fear most the individual who is responsible for their capture.

1. Jack the Ripper

FINDING THE MUTILATED BODY IN MITRE SQARE

"Dear Boss, Grand work the last job was. I gave the lady no time to squeal. How can they catch me now? I love my work and want to start again. You will soon hear of me with my funny little games...My knife's so nice and sharp; I want to get to work right away if I get a chance. Good Luck. Yours truly, Jack the Ripper."

These were excerpts from a letter received by London's Central News Agency on September 27, 1888. It was subsequently transmitted to Scotland Yard, investigating the most notorious killing spree in history. Someone was assaulting women in Whitechapel, murdering them, and then horrifically dismembering their remains.

Jack the Ripper was an unnamed serial murderer who mostly targeted female prostitutes living and working in London's East End slum. Because the killings were never solved, Jack the Ripper became legendary in England. The killings were so well-planned that investigators were unable to determine the killer's gender. He went by many names - the Whitechapel

Murderer, Leather Apron, Saucy Jacky, and, of course, Jack the Ripper. Suppose any other killers in history have inspired so many studies, books, and hypotheses courtesy of police officers, historians, writers, and crime buffs who are collectively known as Ripperologists. In that case, one of them must be Jack the Ripper.

The Autumn of Terror Begins –

Mary Ann Nichols In 1888, the Whitechapel parish in the East End of London was a common place with a crime. It was an overcrowded low-income area with terrible housing and working conditions. There was a brothel on every corner and a bar next to every brothel so the residents may indulge their vices and forget about their poverty-stricken lives. But even for such an area, nobody was prepared for what they were about to discover one early morning on August 31. A man named Charles Cross was on his way to his job on Buck's Row. On the way, he found a woman lying prone in the street, with her skirt raised above her waist. Cross and another man named Robert Paul approached her and touched her head and hands, unable to decide if she was dead or merely unconscious. The two concluded that they should pull down her skirt and that they would alert the first police officer they encountered but, otherwise, they had jobs to get to. The streets of Whitechapel were poorly lit, and it was still night outside. In the darkness, even up-close, neither man noticed that the woman's throat had been slit and her abdomen mutilated. A police constable named John Neil came upon the body, followed closely by Constable Mizen, who had been alerted by Cross. A third constable went to fetch the doctor. The physician pronounced the woman dead and concluded that she had been killed about half an hour prior. This meant that the killer was, likely, still in the area when Charles Cross walked by. The victim was Mary Ann Nichols, a prostitute who also went by "Polly." At first, her murder was linked to a few other killings that we will talk about later. While some blamed a violent gang, the newspapers ran with the story of one deranged killer preying on these women. In the weeks that followed, street gossip created the belief that the killer was a local Jewish man known as "Leather Apron." Whitechapel had a large Jewish population, so resentment against them was high. Of course, the newspapers were more than happy to fuel this sensationalism. The police decided to arrest John Pizer in September, whether it was due to frustration, incompetence, or outside pressure to do something. He was a Polish Jew who worked as a shoemaker, and some said that he was sometimes called "Leather Apron." He also had a prior conviction for a stabbing attack. This was all the police had against Pizer, but, fortunately for him, he had a solid alibi that exculpated him. Pizer even won a libel case against a newspaper that declared him to be the killer.

The Second Murder

Annie Chapman On September 8, the Whitechapel Murderer struck again when the body of Annie Chapman was found in the backyard of Danbury Street by an elderly resident. He flagged down some passing workmen who alerted the police. Chapman's throat had a deep cut, and her body had been mutilated with multiple stab wounds, immediately suggesting a connection with the murder of Mary Nichols. She had been disemboweled, and her intestines had been severed, lifted out of the body and placed on her shoulder. A later post-mortem examination revealed that the killer had removed and taken Chapman's uterus. Dr. George Bagster Phillips examined the wounds and ascertained that a very sharp knife caused them with a long, thin, and narrow blade. It could have been the surgical instrument that a doctor might use for a post-mortem. Phillips also said in his testimony that the murderer showed "indications of anatomical knowledge." These conclusions gave birth to the idea that the killer might be someone with a medical background, a notion that is still pervasive today. The murders caused a huge sensation in London and were discussed in every newspaper in the city.

Meanwhile, the police had to contend with an unexpected problem that significantly impeded their already-plodding investigation. They had to look into hundreds of letters received from the public. Broadly, these missives could be placed into two categories: letters from people offering suggestions or information on how to catch the culprit and letters alleged to be from the killer himself. The police received upwards of 700 letters from the public. Hundreds were purportedly from the Whitechapel Murderer, either taunting or expressing remorse for his actions. You might imagine how this made it almost impossible for the police to ascertain which of the letters, if any, were useful or genuine. That being said, there are a few which many investigators believe in having some merit. The first one we mentioned in the intro of the video. It was sent to the Central News Agency almost 20 days after the murder of Annie Chapman. It starts with the words "Dear Boss" and ends with the murderer giving himself a name. From now on, he is known as Jack the Ripper. The Double Event - Catherine Eddowes and Elizabeth Stride At first, the "Dear Boss" letter was dismissed as a hoax like all the others. However, one particular phrase garnered the interest of the police. When talking about his next job, Jack said that he would "clip the lady's ears off." This became relevant when, just a few days later, the killer did just that.

Elizabeth and Catherine

On September 30, two women fell victim to the Ripper: Elizabeth Stride and Catherine Eddowes. First off was Elizabeth Stride, also known as "Long Liz." She was last seen around midnight in the company of an unidentified man. She was killed soon after that, and her body had already been discovered by 1 a.m. at Dutfield's Yard on Berner Street. Liz died from a long, six-inch gash in her neck but had suffered no mutilations. Because of this, some are still reticent to count her as a Ripper victim, believing that she could have been the target of an unrelated attack. However, others consider enough similarities, such as location and killing method, to group her with the other women. They believe that Jack did not cut up her body because he was either rushing to kill again or, perhaps, because he was interrupted. This is where a Hungarian Jew named Israel Schwartz came in with an interesting story to share, which, if true, meant that he might have been the interrupter. Schwartz told police that he saw a man assault a woman on Berner Street at around 12:45 a.m. that night. Believing he witnessed a domestic spat between husband and wife, he wanted nothing to do with it and crossed the street to avoid them. He later identified Long Liz as the woman he saw that night. His cowardice was subsequently mocked in newspapers that labeled Schwartz a "hen-hearted creature." There are two peculiar details about his story. Firstly, Schwartz claimed that there was a second man in the vicinity smoking a pipe. Secondly, the witness said that the attacker saw him and shouted something at him. Schwartz believed the word was "Lipski", an anti-semitic slur that referenced Israel Lipski, a Jewish man hanged for murder the year before.

Meanwhile, within walking distance of Berner Street, Jack found another victim named Catherine "Kate" Eddowes. After midnight, Kate was walking the streets of London after being released from jail for drunken behavior. She ended up in Mitre Square and was last seen alive at around 1:30 a.m. in the company of a man by three Jewish gentlemen leaving a club on Duke Street. One of those three, Joseph Lawende, got a decent look at the couple and described them, although he mainly remembered their clothes and not their features. Eddowes's body was discovered soon after by a constable walking his beat. Her neck had been cut, and her body suffered gruesome mutilations, more extensive than any previous victims. Her face was disfigured, her intestines were removed and placed on her shoulder again, and the killer had removed her left kidney and part of her uterus. Jack had also cut off Kate's right ear, which is what convinced authorities that the "Dear Boss" letter was the genuine article. More Letters Arrive Speaking of letters, the next day, the Central News Agency received a postcard. The text said:

"I was not codding dear old Boss when I gave you a tip; you'll hear about Saucy Jacky's work tomorrow double event this time number one squealed a bit couldn't finish straight off. I had no time to get ears off for police thanks for keeping the last letter back till I got to work again. Jack the Ripper"

The details and the handwriting suggested to the police not only that the postcard was real, but that the same person wrote it as the "Dear Boss" letter. They published a facsimile in the hope that someone might recognize the handwriting but were unsuccessful. Unfortunately, while it is true that the same person probably wrote both, it is also possible that that person was not Jack the Ripper. Since the start, some investigators believed that these letters were the work of journalists, specifically either Fred Best or Thomas Bulling. They had access to confidential information and wanted to keep Jack interested in alive. Indeed, it is quite feasible that all the correspondence purported to be from Jack the Ripper was written by other people who wanted to be part of the sick charade that surrounded the murders. One more letter merit inclusion, though, because it came with a grisly accessory - part of a human kidney. This message was addressed "From Hell" and was sent to George Lusk, chairman of a volunteer vigilante group called the Whitechapel Vigilance Committee. It read:

"Mr. Lusk, Sir, I send you half the Kidney I took from one woman preserved it for your other piece I fried and ate it was very nice. I may send you the bloody knife that took it out if you only wait a while longer signed Catch me when you can, Mister Lusk" The handwriting in this letter was not the same as the first two. Obviously, the implication was that the kidney belonged to the fourth victim, Catherine Eddowes. Dr. Thomas Openshaw of the London Hospital examined the organ and concluded that it was human. Subsequently, Openshaw received his Ripper letter where Jack lamented that "coppers spoilt the game" and foiled his attempt to claim another victim near Openshaw's hospital.

The Final Victim - *Mary Jane Kelly*

Jack the Ripper saved his most vicious kill for last. His victim was Mary Jane Kelly, an Irish working girl who, at only 25 years old, was much younger than the other murdered women. Also, unlike the rest, she was killed in her home rather than on the street. Kelly's body was discovered on the morning of November 9 at her lodging at 13 Miller's Court by Thomas Bowyer, her landlord's assistant. Bowyer came round to collect the rent and, even though he was a former soldier, he was left stunned by the scene of ineffable horror that awaited him. The first thing he noticed was the broken window. Inside, the room was covered in blood. On the table, he saw piles of meat, not realizing at the moment that they were human flesh. On the bed, there was the body of Kelly, which had been so grotesquely maimed and mangled that it barely looked human anymore. According to the doctor's estimation, it would have taken around two hours to inflict those atrocities upon Mary Kelly. It showed the world just how depraved Jack the Ripper could be when he had all the time and privacy he wanted. Police surgeon Dr. Thomas Bond detailed the extent of her injuries in his report: "The whole of the surface of the abdomen and thighs was removed, and the abdominal cavity emptied of its viscera. The breasts were cut off, the arms mutilated by several jagged wounds, and the face hacked beyond recognition of the features. The tissues of the neck were severed all round to the bone."

The Investigation On the other side of the law, the London police force was engaged in one of the amplest investigations in its history. Thousands of people were interviewed, and hundreds of leads were chased down, yet the public and the media heavily criticized police for failing to apprehend the killer. The inquiry was initially handled by Whitechapel's H Division of the Criminal Investigation Department but was soon taken over by Scotland Yard detectives. Chief among them was Detective Inspector Frederick Abberline, who was put in charge of the case because he previously worked for H Division for 14 years, and it was thought that his local knowledge would prove invaluable. A frequent criticism throughout the investigation concerned police refusal to offer a reward for information. Authorities were accused either of not taking the case seriously or of not caring what happened in a poor district full of immigrants like Whitechapel. In reality, this lack of reward was a new Home Office policy instituted a few years earlier.

The second moment concerns the only clue that Jack the Ripper left following a kill. After he had murdered Catherine Eddowes, he took her apron. Police later found the bloody garment in a stairwell on Goulston Street. Right above it was a piece of graffiti written in chalk that read, "The Juwes are the men that will not be blamed for nothing." Police saw it, copied it down, and wiped it clean on the orders of Police Commissioner Charles Warren. At a time of sky-high racial tensions, he feared that the text might incite a violent riot. Much debate still goes on regarding whether the police acted properly by erasing possible evidence and whether the graffiti was actually a message from Jack the Ripper or just a random anti-Semitic scrawl unconnected to the crimes.

Who Was Jack? Who was Jack the Ripper?

That's the million-dollar question, and historians, scholars, criminologists, authors, and police officers have put forward over a hundred suspects. Inspector Abberline strongly suspected George Chapman, a Polish immigrant and a convicted serial killer who was hanged for three poisonings. Chapman, real name Seweryn Kłosowski, had minor surgical knowledge and arrived in London shortly before the killing spree started. He also left for America in 1891, a few years after the murders stopped. However, Chapman used poison, and criminologists don't believe a killer would change their modus operandi to such an extent. Another convicted serial killer suspected of being Jack was Dr. Thomas Neill Cream. He was also a poisoner, and, according to records, he was in prison in America during the killing spree. All available evidence should dismiss Cream as a candidate, yet he remains a popular choice solely based on the story that Cream's last words allegedly were "I am Jack..." A more plausible suspect was Aaron Kosminski, a Jewish barber who emigrated from Congress Poland sometime in the early 1880s. He was considered a strong candidate by several authorities of that era.

These are just a few of the more sensible suspects. There are many more out there. Some believe the killings were the work of a massonic conspiracy involving the royal family whose goal was to protect Prince Albert Victor. The killer was either the prince himself or the Queen's physician, Sir William Gull. Others opine that the murderer was Lewis Carroll, author of Alice's Adventures in Wonderland, or the post-impressionist painter Walter Sickert. Some believe that Jack the Ripper was, in fact, Jill the Ripper and that the killer was a woman. Ultimately, there isn't sufficient evidence to identify any person as Jack the Ripper beyond a shadow of a doubt. This anonymity surely helped bolster his infamy as here we are, over 100 years after his ghastly killing spree, still talking about it - books, movies, and TV shows that revolve around the Ripper murders are still popular today. So that just leaves us with one question - who do you think was Jack the Ripper?

2. Harold Shipman

Harold Shipman, one of history's most known serial murderers, was a British GP who is thought to have killed over 200 patients before being apprehended by authorities. He was eventually condemned to life in jail for 15 murders but committed himself in prison. The case raised serious questions about the medical community's capabilities and duties in the United Kingdom.

Harold Shipman was a serial murderer and an English medical practitioner. He is regarded as one of history's most prolific serial murderers, having reportedly murdered over 200 of his patients before being apprehended. Shipman was born in England to a middle-class family. He became interested in medicine after witnessing his mother's death from terminal cancer. After graduating from the Leeds School of Medicine, he worked at the Pontefract General Infirmary in Pontefract, West Riding of Yorkshire. He then worked at Donnybrook Medical Centre. Throughout his medical career, he quietly began murdering his patients. In 1998, he was eventually apprehended. Even though he is suspected of killing over 200 people, he was found guilty of just 15 murders and one count of forgery. He received a life sentence with the suggestion that he never be released. He is the only British doctor convicted of murdering his patients, while others have been acquitted on identical allegations. Just a day before his 58th birthday, he committed himself by hanging himself in his cell in Wakefield Prison. Following Shipman's imprisonment, many concerns were raised regarding the capabilities and duties of the British medical community

Dr. Death was a nice and a good guy perfect killing machine. His patients were mainly older women living alone and vulnerable. They adored their doctor Harold Fred Shipman, and even when their contemporaries began dying in unusually high numbers, patients remained loyal. The number of patients Dr. Shipman murdered is still unknown, but his murderous roll call eclipses the toll of any other serial killer caught today.

Did events in his life turn him to murder, or more simply was Harold Shipman born to kill?

Harold Frederick Shipman is an interesting case to examine. The very remarkable nature of his case is that people assumed he couldn't be a killer because he's a bit like a normal guy. Harold Shipman fitted in with society to a great degree, and this was the critical feature that made it possible for him to go on and on to be one of the most prolific serial killers of all time. For his victims, death came in the afternoon, but for Harold Frederick Shipman, it came in the early morning hours at Wakefield prison on Tuesday, January 13, 2004. The expert in death had timed his final act well; he was beyond saving he had been alive at 5 a.m. when the last check was made on him, and he knew the next check was not for another hour as a doctor he also knew that 4 minutes was the maximum time he needed.

What he is done is he's taken to his grave the reason. The motivation behind his killing left everybody guessing about Dutton always perplexed; his suicide caused shockwaves through Hyde, the town in Greater Manchester where most of his victims and their families lived. Hyde was such a lovely town. It was a proper old-fashioned traditional community where sons and daughters still lived on their parent's doorsteps. They all live near each of the males understood each other it was a very close community with a warm heart, so for Shipment to kill so many people in such a small safe community was doubly devastating over the years. Doctors, funeral directors, and pharmacists had raised suspicions about Dr. Shipman, but such worries were swept under the carpet.

Dr. Shipman might have carried on killing for years if it had not been for the suspicious death of Kathleen Grundy on June 24, 1998. The last person to see her alive was Dr. Harold Shipman when he'd gone to her home to take routine blood samples; when Kathleen Grundy died, she left her will that will be made out in favor of dr. Shipman

Kathleen Grundy - Victim

Kathleen Grundy was a vivacious widow with energy to burn and a great love of life. The wealthy 81-year-old had once served as the mayor of Hyde, Lancashire. She was a loved, and respected member of the community noted for her charity work. One of Kathleen's causes was the Age Concern Club, where she helped serve meals to elderly pensioners. She was passionate about this work and known for her punctuality and reliability. So when she didn't show up on June 24, 1998, her friends were immediately concerned. A few of them set off for Kathleen's home, where they found her lying on the sofa fully dressed. When they'd last seen her, she'd been her usual chirpy self. Now she was dead.

Kathleen Grundy had been a patient of Dr. Harold Shipman, who had visited her just a few hours before her death. Mrs. Grundy's friends placed a call to Dr. Shipman, and he arrived soon after and pronounced her dead.

A short while later, Mrs. Grundy's daughter Angela Woodruff got a call from the police, informing her of her mother's death. Angela was stunned. As far as she knew, her mother had been in very good health despite her advanced age. Angela immediately phoned Dr. Shipman for an explanation. The doctor was out, but he later phoned and told Angela that her mother had died of old age. He was also at pains to stress that a postmortem was unnecessary because he had seen her shortly before her death. Lastly, he recommended to Angela that she should have her mother cremated.

Angela Woodruff ignored this last piece of advice and had her buried in keeping with her mother's wishes. Then following the funeral, she received a disturbing call from a firm of solicitors. They claimed to be holding a copy of Mrs. Grundy's last will.

A solicitor herself, Angela had always handled her mother's legal affairs, and as far as she knew, her firm held the original document. She, therefore, set up a meeting to view the new will. The moment she saw the poorly worded, poorly typed document, she knew that it was a fake. "My mother was a meticulously tidy person," she later testified, "the thought of her signing a document which is so badly typed didn't make any sense."

But the shoddy composition of the document was not the only concern. The new will bequeathed all of Kathleen Grundy's worldly possessions to her physician, Dr. Harold Shipman. Angela knew that her mother had liked and respected Shipman, but she could not understand why she'd have left her entire estate to him. She began to suspect that someone had drawn up the document to frame the doctor for Kathleen's death. However, after interviewing the two witnesses to the will, she reluctantly concluded that Dr. Shipman had murdered her mother for money. It was then that she took her suspicions to the police.

The case landed on the desk of Detective Superintendent Bernard Postles, and he quickly drew the same conclusion as Angela Woodruff. The will was quite obviously a forgery and a crude one at that. It cast suspicion on the doctor, especially since Mrs. Grundy had died soon after bequeathed her estate to him. However, to prove murder, a postmortem would have to be carried out. Therefore, an exhumation order was obtained, and hair and tissue samples were taken from the deceased and sent to different labs for analysis.

Meanwhile, the police were concerned that Dr. Shipman might hear of the exhumation and be scared into destroying evidence. They, therefore, launched a raid on the doctor's home and offices, logging into evidence several medical documents and an old typewriter, which would later prove to have been used to type the fake will.

Then the toxicology report arrived, and the police were in for a shock. They had expected that the doctor, with his medical knowledge, would have used a poison that would be difficult to trace - insulin perhaps, which the body produces naturally. Instead, Shipman had injected Mrs. Grundy with a massive dose of morphine, one of the easiest toxins to detect. It pointed to someone confident in his ability to avoid detection, someone perhaps, who'd gotten away with this sort of thing before. Postles began to fear that Kathleen Grundy was not Dr. Shipman's only victim. He'd soon be proven devastatingly correct in that assumption.

The sheer scale of Shipman's killing spree is astonishing. The first murder was believed to have occurred on March 6, 1995, when Shipman injected Marie West with diamorphine. He attributed her death to a stroke. Sixteen months later on July 11, 1996, Shipman visited Irene Turner at her home. Mrs. Turner had recently returned from a holiday and had a cold, for which Shipman administered an injection. The syringe contained morphine, and Mrs. Turner died soon after. He listed the cause of death as diabetes.

On February 28, 1997, a friend of 77-year-old Lizzie Adams arrived for a visit and found Shipman at Ms. Adams' home, and her friend sprawled out on the couch. Shipman claimed that he'd found Ms. Adams in this condition and had just called an ambulance. Then he pretended to make another call canceling the ambulance, saying that the patient had died. Phone records show that neither call was actually made. Shipman recorded the cause of death as pneumonia.

On April 25, 1997, Shipman called on Jean Lilley. When a neighbor saw him leave, she went to check on her friend and found her dead. Shipman claimed that the 59-year-old had died of heart failure, but a pathologist later found the cause of death to be morphine poisoning.

The next to die was 63-year-old Ivy Lomas, killed at Shipman's surgery on May 29, 1997. Two days later, Shipman altered her medical records to fit in with his diagnosis. Mrs. Lomas was a regular at his surgery, and Shipman often referred to her as a nuisance when talking to his staff.

Muriel Grimshaw was found dead at her home on July 14, 1997. Shipman claimed she'd died of a stroke caused by hypertension. He then altered her medical records to support his diagnosis.

On November 28, 1997, Shipman killed Marie Quinn with an injection of morphine. He claimed that Mrs. Quinn had called him saying that she'd just suffered a stroke. He'd rushed to her home, but she was dead when he arrived. Phone records show no calls by Mrs. Quinn to Shipman's surgery on the day in question.

Shipman's next victim was Kathleen Wagstaff, who he claimed had summoned him to her home on December 9, 1997. Records show that no such call was made. He said she had died of heart disease, but no evidence was found of any such illness.

Bianka Pomfret died at her home on December 10, 1997, shortly after a visit from Shipman. He claimed she had died of coronary thrombosis. Forensic experts later found that Shipman had altered the patient's medical records to create a backdated history of heart problems.

Shipman visited Norah Nuttall on January 26, 1998. Less than an hour later, her son arrived to find his mother dead in a chair. Shipman said he had called an ambulance and then canceled it when he realized that Mrs. Nuttall was dead. Phone records showed that neither call was made.

Pamela Hillier, an active 68-year-old, was found dead on February 9, 1998. Shipman said she'd died of a massive stroke. It was later proven that he'd made ten changes to her medical records in order to support his diagnosis.

Maureen Ward, 57, had had cancer but was in remission at the time of her death on February 18, 1998. Shipman recorded her cause of death as a brain tumor, then altered her medical records to suggest that cancer had spread to her brain. A cancer specialist testified at trial that this was not the case and that Mrs. Ward had died from a massive overdose of diamorphine.

Winifred Mellor, 73, was found dead on May 11, 1998, having been visited by Shipman earlier in the day. He claimed she had died of coronary thrombosis and altered her medical records to make it look like she complained of chest pains.

Joan Melia, 73, visited Shipman's surgery on June 12, 1998, suffering from a chest infection. Later that same day, he called her home and claimed to have found her dead. He issued a death certificate citing pneumonia aggravated by emphysema. A pathologist later found evidence of morphine but no serious lung problems.

Harold Shipman, Britain's most prolific serial killer, was behind bars. Yet two questions remained: How many did Shipman kill, and why did he do it?

The answers will likely never be known. However, a public inquiry, chaired by High Court Judge Dame Janet Smith, put the number of victims at 215 (171 women and 44 men, ranging in age from 41 to 93). Another investigation conducted by University of Leicester professor Richard Baker determined that Shipman killed at least 236 of his patients. Either of those numbers makes Shipman the most prolific serial killer in history.

As to why he did it, many contradictory theories have been suggested. Some psychoanalysts speculate that he hated older women; others feel he was re-creating his mother's death in order to satisfy some deep masochistic need. Still, others suggest that he considered himself superior to other people and believed he could do whatever he wanted without fear of discovery. Another theory is that he was fighting a compulsion he simply could not control and that the poorly forged will indicate he desperately wanted to be caught.

An element of truth probably exists in each of these explanations, but perhaps prosecutor Richard Henriques got closest to the answer when he said:

"He was exercising the ultimate power of controlling life and death and repeated the act so often he must have found the drama of taking life to his taste."

We shall never know the whole truth. At around 6 a.m. on Tuesday, January 13, 2004, Harold Shipman was found hanging in his cell at Wakefield prison. He'd committed suicide by fashioning a noose from a bed sheet.

3. John Christie

John Reginald Halliday Christie, often known as Reg Christie by his family and friends, was an English serial murderer and reputed necrophile who operated in the 1940s and early 1950s. He strangled at least eight people, including his wife, Ethel, at 10 Rillington Place in Notting Hill, London. Christie left Rillington Place in March 1953, and the corpses of three of his victims were recovered shortly after in a wallpaper-covered nook in the kitchen. Two more bodies were recovered in the garden, and his wife's body was located beneath the front room floorboards. Christie was caught and convicted of his wife's murder, for which he was sentenced to death by hanging.

Christie was a classic ambiguous serial killer. He was filthy but also fastidious. Christie was a monster that had been going for years and murdering girls left, right and center. There was a sexual element in the killing that gave it a ghoulish glamour in 1953, and the police entered number 10 Rillington place in London. It was simply a house of horror, the scene of eight horrific murders. The man believed to be responsible for these brutal killings was John Reginald Christie.

John Reginald Christie was born in Halifax in 1899, one of seven children. He was the youngest male amongst a largely female household, and he resented the fact the girls in the family had power over him. It made him crave the opportunity for Authority. As a child, he had few friends, although he did participate in sports and boy scouts. When Christie was eight, his paternal grandfather died, and he was allowed to view the body, an experience that seemed to affect him profoundly.

Leaving school at the age of fifteen, he got a job as a projectionist in a movie theater. Then World War I arrived, and he was drafted, becoming a signalman. He only saw action once during his service, suffering a mustard gas attack that temporarily blinded him. He also lost his voice and remained without the power of speech for three years. Doctors who examined Christie determined that this was a hysterical reaction rather than due to physical damage. This would prove a lifelong pattern for Christie, who often feigned or exaggerated illness to avoid difficult situations.

After his discharge from the army, Christie got a job as a clerk. In 1920 he married Ethel Simpson Waddington, despite being mostly speechless during the courtship. The marriage remained unconsummated for over two years due to Christie's inability to perform with his wife. He did, however, frequent prostitutes during this time, something he'd done since the age of 19.

Christie became a postman early in the marriage, but he was fired after being caught stealing postal orders. He was sentenced to three months in prison. Upon his release, he abandoned Ethel in Sheffield and absconded to London. Christie held a series of short-term jobs over the next four years before finding himself sentenced to a prison term of nine months, again for theft. After being released from that stint, he lived for a time with a prostitute but was again in trouble after he attacked the woman with a cricket bat. Another spell of incarceration followed a few years later for stealing a car.

Christie had by this time been separated from his wife for almost ten years, but after his release, he contacted Ethel and asked for reconciliation. Lonely and starved for attention, Ethel agreed and joined Christie in London in 1933. Not long after the reunion, Christie was hit by a car and had to be hospitalized. This only exacerbated his hypochondria. He regularly stayed off work and, over the next 15 years, would pay almost 200 visits to various doctors.

Christie became involved with a local prostitute Ruth; first was an Austrian emigrated. She came over to this country to train as a nurse, but by the time she met Christie in 1943, she's selling sexual services to American Air Force Minh. In other words, she's working as a prostitute. With Christie's wife away, Ruth became a regular visitor to his ground floor flat, where he paid for her services. Christie gets a telegram from his wife saying she's coming back from Sheffield, and since he doesn't want to take the chance of Ruth exposing him to his wife Ethel, he thinks he'll have to dispose of Ruth. Just during their final sexual encounter, Christie strangled Ruth. So, clearly, this is the beginning of that sexual fetish that he has emerging Christy's first murder had given him a thrill; he was soon looking for another victim to satisfy his desires

Christie carried on without a care in the world; he'd given up his job as a special constable and was now working at the ultra radio works in Acton. It was there that he met Muriel Edie came from a respectable family spinster in her 30s. They met regularly in the canteen over a meal, and she grew to trust him, and she had this problem with a guitar. She talked about that, and that sort of set his mind rolling. With his wife away, Christie offered to cure Muriel of her affliction using a breathing device. When she visited 10 Rillington place, he put a mask on her face, and it was connected to the gas. The gas will render Muriel Edie unconscious for him to have control as opposed to a living, breathing woman who will have her own views about what might be happening in terms of their relationship. With his victim unconscious, Christie had sex with Muriel, and then he produced a rope and strangled her. Christie had now taken the lives of two young women, Ruth fewest and Muriel Edie; he buried their bodies in his back garden.

Nobody knew they'd been visiting Christie, which meant he was free to continue his murder spree, and it wouldn't take him long to strike again. Christie hid behind an air of respectability working as a ledger Clark at the post office. It's alleged that he and his wife Ethel also helped out women who found themselves with unwanted pregnancies. In 1948 a couple by the name of Evans moved into the flat above the Christie's. Tim and Beryl Evans were expecting their first child, and they quickly attracted the attention of their sinister neighbor. This young couple moved from

Wales. Tim is from Wales, moves into London trying to get a job. This is a young man in his mid-20s newly married working as a van driver and crucially has an IQ reputedly to be around 70, and he's got this wife as well. Still, Christie clearly is interested because of course that Chris is interested sexually in young women that he can have power over. The Evanses had their first baby Geraldine, but family life wasn't all they'd hoped it would be; the cramped and squalid conditions of railings in place weren't ideal for raising a child. The problem came when she conceived a second child, and suddenly panic set in they were all short of money; he was earning seven pounds a week. He could make it up to eight pounds, but then that had to cover the payments on whether rental the payments on the furniture and all the other things unknown to Beryl. John Christie had learned of her situation and was preparing a way to solve Barrel's problem. Beryl is panicking; she wants to have an abortion; first of all, her husband was against it, so she tries to give herself an abortion by taking pills inevitably. Christy got to hear about it and said look I can solve this problem you know and Evans went along with the notion that Christy would go up and perform this in fact he came down his wife said when he go downstairs tell Christy it's all right which he did then he went off to work little did Timothy Evans know he was leaving his wife in the hands of a murderer on his return Evans was told by Christy that he'd tried to carry out an abortion on Beryl but tragically she'd died during the procedure when Timothy comes back from work that particular evening Christy reveals his your wife has died and you're to blame he said to Evans well of course I go to prison but you know so will you because you're an accessory so what we have to do is cover this up barrels body was dumped into an empty room in 10 Rillington place Christy told him he'd get rid of her body down a manhole outside Evans was now left looking after his baby and having to explain the disappearance of her mother with an IQ well below the average of 100 Evans was susceptible to another idea from his neighbor Christy

so Christy said I've got a childless couple East Acton who would take the child on and see that she was properly brought up and you could go back and see her you know eventually of course these people didn't exist but far as Evans were concerned they did the key thing that Christy would be telling Evans is that you have to get out of London but don't imagine that Timothy Evans is going to behave logically Timothy Evans was a young man clearly stressed clearly doesn't know how to react and is listening to somebody who he thinks is looking out for his best interests so he simply does as he's told with his beloved wife dead it's believed Evans made the decision to leave his child in the care of Christie he then fled to Wales to stay with relatives both Beryl and Tim's family started to ask questions about his wife and child's whereabouts on the 30th of November unable to maintain the pretense any longer and wracked with guilt Tim went to the police station and he made the first of the two statements in method did Ville the first said my wife died in an abortion and I disposed of her down the manhole outside the police visited remains in place searched the manhole and found nothing if they'd looked elsewhere they might have found the hidden bodies of Christie's victims at this point Evans implicated Christie claiming he'd played a part in her death in his statement of the police he said I asked him how long she'd been dead he said since 3 o'clock then he told me my wife's stomach had been septic poisoned the police paid another visit to rulings in place and this time knocked on the door of John Christie the Christie's presented a united front denying any wrongdoing the word of this respectable middle-aged couple appeared to be worth more than that of working-class Evans but of course you've got a young man who's disappeared as of London and then reports his wife as being murdered he tells the police she's going to be found in a particular drain that's a lie so the police don't have any reason to believe Timothy Evans Christie told the police that his neighbour Evans was an abusive alcoholic the police quickly established that barrel and the baby were missing and carried out a full-scale search of Rillington place behind a woodpile in the washhouse they uncovered the remains of Tim's wife Beryl and most shockingly that a baby Geraldine they'd both been strangled but the suspicion of guilt didn't fall upon Christie he was taken to see the bodies at the mortuary and but he was shocked by the fact that his daughter was dead because he'd come back firmly believing that Geraldine was still alive and he came up with the story about you know where they've gone to people in in East Acton after a lengthy interrogation at Notting Hill police station the easily led Evans changed his story once again he confessed to the murders of his wife and child

Christie had a ready excuse for each of the murders. Of his wife, he said that he'd woken up to find her blue in the face and choking. He tried to resuscitate her but was unable to do so he decided to end her suffering by strangling her. He'd later found an empty pill bottle and assumed that Ethel had tried to kill herself. The other three women were also "not his fault." He said he'd met Rita Nelson on the street on January 19, 1953. She allegedly demanded money from him, saying she'd scream and accuse him of attacking her if he didn't give her 30 shillings. He walked away, but she followed him back to his house, forcing her way in. She then picked up a frying pan and tried to hit him. They struggled, and she fell back on a chair that had a rope hanging from it. Christie blacked out and woke up to find her dead.

In February, he met Kathleen Maloney, 26, in a Notting Hill café. Learning that she was searching for a flat, he offered to help. Kathleen went home with Christie, but once there, she threatened violence if he didn't use his influence with the landlord to get her a flat. He blacked out, and when he revived, she was dead. He did not remember killing her.

Of Hectorina MacLennan, Christie said that he gave her and her boyfriend a place to stay. However, after a few days, he asked them to leave. Hectorina later returned alone. Christie tried to get her to leave, and they struggled. After a while, she went limp and sank to the floor. Christie believed that some of her clothing might have got wrapped around her neck and choked her. He later told a different version of events, one that rings truer. He said he invited Hectorina to his house for a drink. Once there, he got her to sit in a chair over which he'd constructed a special canopy. He then turned on the gas. Hectorina tried to leave, but he caught her at the door and throttled her into unconsciousness. He'd then had sex with her before finishing her off with the gas.

Confronted with evidence regarding the murders of Ruth Fuerst and Muriel Eady, he readily admitted to killing them, although he denied murdering Beryl

Evans and her daughter. Later he admitted to killing Beryl but denied killing Geraldine. (Ludovic Kennedy firmly believes that Christie killed the baby but that the act was so traumatic that he wiped it from his memory.

Christie was held at Brixton prison pending his trial. He was examined by several psychiatrists who registered a universal dislike for the man, describing him as "nauseating" and "sniveling." He had a habit of dropping his voice to a whisper whenever he was asked a question that he did not like. He also spoke of himself in the third person as though dissociating himself from his deeds. With the other inmates, though, it was a different story. Christie boasted about his deeds, comparing himself to the infamous acid bath killer John George Haigh, murderer of six people. Christie said that he had planned on outdoing Haigh by killing 12.

John Reginald Christie went on trial at the Old Bailey on June 22nd, 1953. His defense pleaded him Not Guilty because of Insanity and produced expert witnesses to testify as to the integrity of this. The prosecution produced their own witnesses to testify that Christie was sane and therefore guilty. The trial lasted only four days, and the jury deliberated for only an hour and 20 minutes before pronouncing Christie guilty. He was sentenced to death. Christie did not appeal and went to the gallows at Pentonville Prison on July 15, 1953.

Yet, that was not the end of the case. In the wake of Christie's trial, many now believed that the state had hanged Timothy Evans, innocent man. An inquiry was hastily convened and after just 11 days concluded that Evans had indeed strangled his wife and baby. However, this verdict was unsatisfactory to many observers. Two years later, a delegation of four press editors approached the Home Secretary to request another inquiry. Their request was denied, as was a subsequent application.

Eventually, in 1965 a new inquiry was conducted. It reached a strange conclusion, deciding that Evans had strangled his wife but not his daughter. As Evans had been tried only for the murder of his daughter, High Court Judge Sir Daniel Brabin granted him a posthumous pardon in 1966. This did not declare him innocent, only innocent of the charge for which he was tried – the murder of his daughter. However, the evidence suggests that Christie killed both Beryl and Geraldine and the six other women found concealed at 10 Rillington Place.

4. Graham Young

In February 1961, a peculiar illness started afflicting the young household in north London. It began with 37-year-old Molly Young suffering bouts of vomiting and diarrhea, along with excruciating stomach pains. Then her husband Fred, 44, began experiencing similar symptoms, and Fred's daughter Winifred, 22, also became violently ill. Finally, at 14, the youngest member of the family, Graham, succumbed to the mystery bug. And it didn't stop there. Before long, the affliction had spread beyond the immediate family. Several of Graham's school friends were ill with similarly painful symptoms.

For nine long months, the young family endured their illness, passing various theories as to its source. Then in November 1961, things took a more serious turn. Winifred Young was on her way to work when she began suffering hallucinations and had to be rushed from the train to the hospital. The doctors who examined her were mystified - Winifred appeared to have been poisoned with a rare form of Belladonna.

The doctors may have been puzzled, but it immediately made sense to him when Fred Young heard the prognosis. His son Graham was obsessed with chemistry and was always messing around with some or other concoction. It now seemed clear to Fred that Graham had somehow, inadvertently, contaminated the family's food.

He confronted his son with this theory, but Graham denied it. He blamed Winifred, who he said had been mixing shampoo in the family's teacups. Unconvinced, Fred searched Graham's room but found nothing incriminating. Nevertheless, he warned his son to be more careful in the future.

Graham's interest in chemistry had begun at an early age. He was not yet 10- years old when he'd begun stealing his stepmother's nail varnish and perfumes to analyze the contents. By 11, he could recite the components of various headache pills and cough medicines and would joyously warn of the symptoms of overdosing on them. He spent hours at the library poring over books on his favorite subject. By the time he was 13, Graham had already acquired a level of knowledge similar to that of a chemistry post-graduate.

But Graham's fascination with chemistry went beyond mere schoolboy inquisitiveness. He had a particular interest in poisons, was known to carry a bottle of acid with him, and had once constructed a bomb that had destroyed a neighbor's wall. Still, Fred couldn't believe that his son would deliberately be poisoning his family. Before long, he'd have cause to re-evaluate that belief.

Graham Young was born in Neasden, northwest London, on September 7, 1947. His mother, Margaret developed pleurisy during the pregnancy, and although she delivered a healthy baby, she died of tuberculosis just three months after the birth. Devastated by her death and unable to cope with two young children, Fred Young sent Graham to live with his Aunt Winnie while her grandmother took 8-year-old Winifred in.

Then when Graham was two-and-a-half, Fred remarried and reunited his family, this time with their new stepmother Molly.

We will never know what effect these early upheavals may have had on the boy, but Graham Young showed signs that he was different from an early age. Other boys idolized football players and pop stars; his heroes were murderers like Crippen and William Palmer. Where other kids read comic books and teen magazines, his favorite reading was "Sixty Famous Trials," especially the chapters on infamous poisoners.

If that wasn't enough, he began developing an unhealthy interest in the Nazis. From the age of about 12, he began talking openly about his admiration for Adolf Hitler. He also became fascinated with the occult and claimed to be part of a local coven run by a man he had met at the library.

At school, Graham was a solitary child. Most of his classmates found him "creepy," while he hardly endeared himself to teachers by wearing a swastika badge on his uniform. World War II had ended only 15 years before; wounds were still fresh for many who had lost friends and loved ones.

Graham was an intelligent boy, but he showed little interest in his studies. The one exception was chemistry, in which his fascination bordered on obsession. Most afternoons, he could be found at the library poring over books on the subject, particularly ones on toxicology, the study of poisons.

Graham spent much of his time alone in his room, dabbling with one or another experiment at home. His relationship with his father appears distant, while he openly admitted to his classmates how much he hated his stepmother. He'd show them a small plasticize figure stuck full of pins and claim it was a voodoo doll representing Molly. On one occasion, after Molly reprimanded him for some or other infraction, he drew a picture of a tombstone on which he wrote: "In

Hateful Memory of Molly Young, RIP." He then deliberately left it out where she would see it.

The first person to be subjected to Graham Young's experiments with poison was a boy named Christopher Williams, who had befriended Young due to a mutual interest in science. Williams was a neighbor of the Young family, and he and Graham would often eat lunch together at school, sometimes swapping sandwiches. It wasn't long before Christopher began suffering from headaches, vomiting, and painful stomach cramps. His mother at first thought he was play-acting in order to stay home from school, but eventually, she took him to a doctor, who diagnosed a migraine. No one considered poison; after all, how would a 13-year-old get his hands on dangerous toxins?

Graham Young had though, using his detailed knowledge of poisons to convince two local pharmacists that he was 17 and needed the substances for his studies. Using this ruse, he built up a substantial stash of antimony, arsenic, digitalis and thallium – enough it was later calculated to kill 300 people.

Still, he stuck to relatively small doses with Christopher Williams, and despite Williams knowing about his friend's obsession with poisons, he apparently never suspected him. For his part, Graham did a good job of playing the concerned buddy, even if he seemed overly eager to hear Christopher's descriptions of his pain and suffering.

Luckily for Williams, Young soon tired of torturing him. The problem was that Christopher's frequent absences from school made it impossible for Graham to monitor his symptoms. He needed subjects which he could observe at close quarters, so he turned his attention to those nearest to him - his own family.

During the early months of 1962, Molly Young's health deteriorated steadily. She lost weight, suffered excruciating backache, and began losing her hair. She also appeared to age noticeably. Then her symptoms changed suddenly. On Easter Saturday 1962, she woke up with stiffness in her neck muscles and the sensation of pins and needles in her hands and feet. Despite feeling unwell, Molly went out shopping while Fred Young went for a drink at the local pub. When Fred returned home at around lunchtime, he found Graham standing transfixed at the kitchen window, staring out into the back garden. Following his son's gaze, Fred saw Molly writhing in agony on the grass. She died in hospital later that day.

Molly Young's death was put down to the prolapse of a bone at the top of the spinal column (a common symptom of antimony poisoning, although no one seemed to make the connection at the time). However, it would later emerge that this was not the cause of death. Graham had in fact, been feeding antimony to Molly for so long that she'd built up a tolerance to the poison. Frustrated that the antimony was no longer having any effect, Young changed his poison of choice.

On the night prior to her death, he'd spiked Molly's evening meal with 20 grains of thallium, a colorless, odorless, tasteless 'heavy metal.' He overdid it somewhat – 20 grams is enough to kill five people.

One might think that the death of his stepmother would have frightened Graham out of conducting further 'experiments,' instead, it seems to have spurred him on. Several of the extended Young family suffered vomiting and diarrhea after eating the sandwiches provided after the funeral. And Graham had already switched his attention to his next victim – his grieving father.

Fred Young had suffered occasional vomiting, diarrhea, and stomach cramps during Molly's illness, but after her death, the symptoms intensified to such an extent that he eventually had to be hospitalized. Graham visited him frequently but spent most of his time enthusiastically discussing Fred's condition and symptoms with the doctors. Eventually, antimony poisoning was diagnosed. But if Fred suspected that

Graham was responsible, he didn't say. The idea that his own son might be the cause of his torment (and possibly the death of his wife) must have been too horrendous to contemplate.

It took an outsider to draw the authorities' attention to Graham Young. Geoffrey Hughes, Graham's chemistry teacher, had long been uneasy about the boy's behavior and bizarre utterings. Eventually, he decided to search Graham's desk and was shocked at what he found there – bottles of poisons, juvenile sketches of dying men, essays about infamous poisoners. Hughes took his findings to the police.

A few days later, Young was called into what he thought was a careers interview. In reality, the interviewer (in reality a police psychiatrist) began by asking Young about his interests and then encouraged him to talk about his expertise with poisons. Needless to say, Young took to this like a duck to water, leaving the interviewer shocked and horrified with some of his pronouncements.

Yet when the true intent of the interview was revealed, Young initially denied everything. Eventually, though, he broke down and confessed before leading officers to his various caches of poisons.

Although there was insufficient evidence to try the 14-year-old for the murder of his stepmother, he was convicted of poisoning his father, sister, and friend Chris Williams. He was sent to Broadmoor maximum-security hospital with an order that he was not to be released without the permission of the Home Secretary for 15 years. He would be the youngest inmate to be incarcerated at Broadmoor since 1885.

And he soon made his mark. A few weeks after his arrival at the hospital, a fellow prisoner named John Berridge died of cyanide poisoning. Young had been heard complaining about Berridge and his loud snoring in the communal dorms. The authorities were baffled. There was no cyanide anywhere in prison, so how had Berridge ingested it? Young was quick to enlighten them. He said that cyanide could be extracted from laurel bush leaves, and there are plenty growing in the adjoining fields. It sounded suspiciously like a confession, but for whatever reason, it wasn't followed up. Berridge's death was ruled a suicide.

A number of other suspicious incidents occurred during Young's stay at Broadmoor. On one occasion, the staff's coffee was found to be contaminated with bleach; on another, a quantity of toxic sugar soap (a substance used to wash down walls prior to painting) was found in a tea urn.

Young also kept up his earlier interest in Nazism, growing a Hitler mustache and making hundreds of wooden swastikas. While these hardly appear the actions of a man working towards ridding himself of the demons that plagued him, Young was in other respects a model prisoner. After serving five years, he was moved to a less secure block. At eight years, the prison psychiatrist Dr. Edgar Udwin petitioned the Home Secretary for his release, stating confidently that

Young was "no longer obsessed with poisons, violence, and mischief."

Sensing his imminent release, Young wrote to his sister Winifred, joking: "Your friendly neighborhood Frankenstein will soon be at liberty." To one of the Broadmoor nurses, he said: "When I get out, I'm going to kill one person for every year I've spent in this place."

Incredibly this apparently genuine threat never reached the ears of the authorities. Young was released on February 4, 1971. After staying with Winifred and her husband Dennis for a week, Young moved to a hostel in Slough. Soon after his arrival, fellow resident Trevor Sparkes, 34, began experiencing sharp pains in his stomach. Young suggested that a glass of wine might help, but this only made things worse. Sparkes began vomiting and suffering diarrhea. His face swelled, and he began experiencing pains in his scrotum. Eventually, Sparkes collapsed while playing a game of soccer. He was rushed to the hospital, but doctors couldn't diagnose the problem. He continued suffering terrible pains for years after. Another hostel dweller began experiencing similar symptoms after going out for a drink with Young. This man endured such agonizing pain that he ended up taking his own life.

Young meanwhile had found employment as a store clerk at John Hadland Ltd, a photographic company in Bovingdon, Hertfordshire. In lieu of references, he referred his new employer to Dr. Udwin, the Broadmoor psychiatrist. Udwin wrote back with assurances that Young had made a full recovery from the personality disorder that had plagued him. No mention was made of his love of poisons, which is astounding given the many toxic chemicals stored on the premises of his new employer.

As it turned out, Young did not need the toxins available on site. He had already armed himself with a stash of antimony and thallium, obtained using a fake ID, from a London pharmacist.

Young made friends quickly at Hadland, first with 41-year-old Ron Hewitt, whose job he was taking over, then with 59-year-old storeroom manager Bob Egle and 60-year-old stock supervisor Fred Biggs. It wasn't long before Egle started feeling ill and began to take time off work. Then Ron Hewitt developed diarrhea, sharp abdominal pains, and a burning sensation in the throat after drinking a cup of tea brought to him by Young. The symptoms subsided after a few days at home but resumed immediately after he returned to work.

Hewitt left the company soon after and suffered no further symptoms. Bob Egle, too, recovered after taking a holiday. However, the day after returning to work, the mystery illness was back. His fingers became numb, and he couldn't move without agonizing pain. By the time he was rushed to the hospital, he was virtually paralyzed and unable to speak. He died ten days later on July 7, 1971, the cause of death given as bronchial pneumonia.

Of all the Hadland employees, Graham Young seemed most affected by Egle's death, so much so that he was chosen to accompany the managing director to the cremation.

In the weeks following the death, the staff at Hadland tried to put the tragic incident behind them. However, Young seemed unprepared to let it go. He mused endlessly about the possible medical causes of Egle's symptoms. Then in September 1971, Fred Biggs began to suffer similar symptoms. And the illness also spread to other staff members.

One of Young's colleagues in the storeroom Jethro Batt, 39, accepted a cup of coffee from Young one evening but threw it away because it tasted bitter. "What's the matter?" Young smirked. "Do you think I'm trying to poison you?" A short while later, Batt started throwing up and experienced intense pain in his legs. Peter Buck and David Tilson also suffered. Batt and Tilson started losing clumps of hair, giving them the appearance, in the words of a doctor, of "three-quarter plucked chickens."

Other staff members displayed different symptoms. Receptionist Diana Smart complained of suffering from foul-smelling feet, while Buck and Tilson found themselves rendered impotent. These and other ailments were put down to some kind of virus that became known locally as "the Bovingdon Bug." Several residents had indeed been afflicted with a stomach bug over the preceding few months, and this provided Young with a fortuitous cover.

After toning down his activities for a short while, the poisoner was back with a vengeance. Jethro Batt fell ill again, his pain so extreme that he had to be hospitalized. Fred Biggs suffered even worse symptoms, his skin began to peel off, and he was in so much pain that he could not stand the weight of a bed sheet on his body. When death finally came on November 19, it must have seemed a merciful release.

The company directors were at a loss to explain what had killed two employees in such a short time. On the afternoon that Fred Biggs' death was announced, they brought in a doctor to assure staff that there was no evidence that hygiene on the company premises could have caused the deaths and illnesses. Yet even as the doctor concluded his statement, a hand shot up at the back of the room. Graham Young wanted to know whether the doctor had considered thallium poisoning a possible cause and provided a detailed explanation of why he thought this might be the case. The doctor was puzzled by Young's questions and told the company's managing director about them. He, in turn, informed the police.

It didn't take long for detectives to figure out that the outbreak of illnesses had started shortly after Young had begun working at Hadland. A brief conversation with their forensic colleagues confirmed that the victims' symptoms were consistent with thallium poisoning. A quick background check uncovered

Graham Young's past as a convicted poisoner. A search of Young's room turned up bottles, vials, and tubes of various poisons plus a ledger in which Young had cataloged in great detail the sufferings and symptoms of his subjects, even including graphs to determine when they might expire. The day before Fred Biggs died, an entry read: "'F' is responding to treatment. He is obstinately difficult. If he survives a third week, he will live. I am most annoyed."

On Saturday, November 21, 1971, Young was visiting his father and Aunt Winnie in Sheerness, Kent, when police officers arrived to arrest him. After they had left with Graham in custody, Fred Young gathered Graham's birth certificate and every other document relating to his son and tore them to shreds.

Under interrogation, Young quickly confessed to the poisonings. He even boasted of having committed "the perfect murder" of his stepmother in 1962. He refused to sign a statement admitting his guilt, though. He was intent on having his day in court and of exploiting his notoriety to the full

Graham Young went on trial at St. Albans Crown Court in June 1972. Young was confident, cocky even, believing he couldn't be prosecuted because Bob Egle had been cremated, thus destroying evidence of thallium poisoning. In the case of Fred Biggs, he insisted that he'd given Fred some thallium grains to help him kill bugs in his garden. Biggs must have ingested those accidentally. He also explained away the diary, claiming it was research he was doing for a novel he planned to write.

But Young reckoned without advances in forensic science. Experts were able to find traces of thallium in Bob Egle's ashes. Fred Biggs' wife also confirmed that he never used thallium on his garden, while Young's claim about the diary being a research document was proven to be ludicrous, given some of the excerpts.

Young was convicted of two murders, two attempted murders, and two counts of administering poison. He was sentenced to four terms of life imprisonment and served in the maximum-security Parkhurst prison. He died there in 1990, aged just 42. The cause of death was a heart attack, although many believe that he managed to poison one final victim - himself.

5. Peter Tobin

Peter Britton Tobin was born on August 27, 1946, in Johnstone, Renfrewshire, the youngest of seven children. He showed early signs of aberrant behavior, and at the age of just seven, he was sent to a special school for difficult children. Not that the school did much to change his conduct, he'd barely been released when he was arrested on charges of burglary and sent to a juvenile institution. He'd serve numerous terms in reformatories, eventually graduating to an adult prison in 1970, when he was convicted on burglary and forgery charges.

Tobin was by then living in England, having moved to Brighton in 1969. He was also married, but Margaret Mountney divorced him in 1971, citing spousal abuse. He'd marry twice more and father three children. However, each of these marriages would end in divorce, the women always telling a similar story. Tobin would start charming and attentive but soon turn to sadistic violence.

In August 1993, Tobin was living in the town of Havant, Hampshire. On August 4, he hired two 14-year old girls to babysit his son. He then forced the girls at knifepoint to drink vodka and cider before sexually assaulting and raping them.

Tobin warned the girls not to report the incident, but he took precautions anyway. By the time the police arrived to arrest him, he was long gone, having fled to a religious retreat in nearby Warwickshire. He lived there for months under an assumed name but was identified after the BBC ran a segment about his case on its Crime Watch program.

Brought before Winchester Crown Court on May 18, 1994, Tobin pleaded guilty and received a 14-year prison term. He served ten and was released in 2004; he moved to Paisley in his native Scotland. In May 2007, he was back in prison, serving 30 months for breaching the conditions of his parole.

Given the trajectory Peter Tobin's life was on, it seems inevitable that he'd eventually graduate to murder. In September 2006, he worked as a handyman at St. Patrick's Roman Catholic Church in Glasgow. Once again, in contravention of his parole, he'd taken on an assumed name, "Pat McLaughlin."

At that time, a 23-year-old Polish student named Angelika Kluk was living at the chapel, working part-time as a cleaner to finance her studies. Kluk was last seen alive on September 24, 2006. Five days later, her brutalized body was discovered hidden under some floorboards in the church. She'd been beaten, raped, and stabbed to death. Forensic evidence would later suggest that she was still alive when her body was placed under the floor.

"Pat McLaughlin," meanwhile, was nowhere to be found. He'd fled to London and checked himself into a hospital under yet another alias. He was arrested there a few days later.

Peter Tobin went on trial at the Edinburgh High Court in March 2007. Found guilty of rape and murder, he was sentenced to life in prison with the stipulation that he must serve at least 21 years before being eligible for parole.

However, the story of Peter Tobin doesn't end there. The police had long suspected him in the 1991 disappearance of a 15-year-old girl named Vicky Hamilton. On February 10, 1991, Vicky was last seen waiting for a bus in Bathgate, West Lothian. Tobin had been living in the town at the time, but true to his usual M.O., he'd moved away days after Vicky's disappearance.

In July 2007, the police searched Tobin's house and announced soon after that they'd charged a man in connection with Vicky Hamilton's death. They searched another of Tobin's former homes in England in early October, where he'd fled after leaving Bathgate.

On November 14, 2007, the police announced that remains found buried in the back garden of a house in Margate, Kent, Vicky Hamilton. They also confirmed that the body of another young woman (later identified as Dinah McNicol) had also been discovered.

Tobin went on trial for Vicky Hamilton's murder in December 2008. Found guilty, he was sentenced to an additional life term.

On December 14, 2009, he was back in court charged with the murder of Dinah McNicol. Dinah had last been seen alive on August 5, 1991, when she was hitchhiking home from a music festival in the company of a male companion. A driver had picked them up and later dropped the man off while Vicky remained in the car. She was never seen alive again. In the days after her disappearance, regular withdrawals continued to be made from her bank account.

The jury took less than 15 minutes to convict Tobin of Dinah McNicol's murder. A third life term was tacked onto his sentence, with the judge recommending that Tobin never be released.

The three murders he has been convicted for are unlikely to be the full extent of Tobin's killing spree. The police have since assembled a task force to investigate 13 more homicides in which his involvement is suspected. At the same time, Tobin privately boasts to his fellow inmates that he has committed 48 murders.

There is also evidence to suggest that Tobin might be Bible John, an as yet unidentified serial killer who terrorized Glasgow during the late sixties. Tobin was living in the area when Bible John claimed his three victims, and a police sketch drawn up from eyewitness accounts bears a remarkable resemblance to him. Coincidentally, the Bible John killings ended after Tobin left Scotland in 1969

6. William Palmer

The case of William Palmer is one of the most notorious in British legal history. Born in the town of Rugeley, Staffordshire, on August 6, 1824, Palmer took to crime at an early age. By the time he was 17 he had already been accused of a number of offenses, ranging from embezzlement to running an abortion service. He was also suspected of poisoning a drinking companion, and although nothing could be proven, he was dismissed from his medical internship.

Overcoming these setbacks, Palmer qualified as a doctor from St Bartholomew's Hospital in 1846. Thereafter he settled down to a modest practice in his hometown and in 1847 wed Ann Thornton at St. Nicholas Church, Abbots Bromley. Their first son William Brookes Palmer was born a year later, in 1848.

From the outside, Palmer appeared to be living the life of a respectable small-town doctor. The truth was somewhat different. Local gossip had it that Palmer had several mistresses, including some of his servant girls. He also had a serious gambling problem and was deeply in shock due to money lost on card games and horse racing.

The first of several suspicious deaths connected to Palmer occurred on January 18, 1849, when his mother-in-law Ann Mary Thornton died suddenly while visiting the Palmer household. Mrs. Thornton was only 50 years old at the time and in good health, yet her death seems to have aroused no suspicion. Palmer's wife inherited a considerable sum from the estate.

Sixteen months later, on May 10, 1850, another houseguest of the Palmers, Leonard Bladen, died. And over the next four years, the household appeared cursed as four of the Palmer children died in infancy.

There were other suspicious deaths too. Joseph Bentley, an elderly uncle of Palmer, died on October 27, 1852, his passing attracting no attention from the authorities. Not even the death of Palmer's wife Ann, just 27 years old when she suddenly became ill and died, aroused much suspicion. Palmer was carrying on an affair with one of his maids at the time. She later bore him an illegitimate son. The child, like so many of Palmer's offspring, did not survive infancy.

Palmer had taken out a life insurance policy on his wife, and her death brought him the considerable sum of £13 000. But even that was not enough to service his gambling debt. He needed more money and soon turned his deadly attentions to his brother. Walter Palmer was insured for £10 000 and died on August 16, 1855. However, the insurance company refused to pay out, claiming that not enough time had elapsed since the purchase of the policy. And there was a further setback for Palmer when one of his former lovers, the daughter of a Staffordshire police officer, began blackmailing him.

Heavily in debt, Palmer set off for the Shrewsbury Horse Races on November 13, 1855. However, if he was hoping for a change of luck, it did not materialize. He lost heavily over the three days of the meeting.

Palmer's companion at the races, John Parsons Cook, had considerably better luck and invited Palmer for a celebratory drink at a pub called "The Raven." Palmer reciprocated by inviting Cook to dinner at his house on November 17. Immediately after, Cook began complaining of feeling ill. Within a short, while he was so poorly that Palmer insisted he stays until he had recovered. Ever the good friend, he even stated his commitment to personally nurse Cook back to health.

The next day a housemaid at the Palmer residence sampled a broth that Palmer had prepared for Cook. A short while later, she was violently ill. Palmer, meanwhile, had departed for London to collect the money Cook had won at the races. He was back on November 19. On November 21, John Cook was dead.

Cook's stepfather, a Mr. Stevens, was the executor of his estate and was immediately suspicious of the circumstances surrounding his stepson's death. He called for an autopsy; the examination was completed on November 26. In early December, a coroner's inquest was held and delivered a unanimous verdict of "death by willful murder."

The obvious suspect was William Palmer. Yet, there was very little evidence to connect him with the crime. Indeed Palmer would likely have gotten away with it had he not tried to bribe several people involved with the inquest. That aroused suspicion, and when it was learned that Palmer had bought a quantity of strychnine just before Cook's death, he was placed under arrest.

Shortly after Palmer was detained, the bodies of his wife and brother were exhumed. However, there was not enough evidence to charge Palmer with murder in their deaths. Not that the prosecution needed it. They believed that they had a strong enough case against Palmer for the murder of John Cook.

Palmer went on trial at London's Old Bailey in May 1856, the trial having been moved due to the ill-feeling towards him in his native Staffordshire. The evidence was largely circumstantial, but it was enough for the jury to find him guilty of murder. (Many modern legal scholars believe that the evidence was insufficient to convict him.

Palmer went to the gallows outside Stafford Prison on June 14, 1856, watched by a raucous crowd of some 30,000. As he stepped onto the platform, Palmer is said to have examined the trapdoor and remarked to the executioner, "Are you sure it's safe?"

7. Beverley Allitt

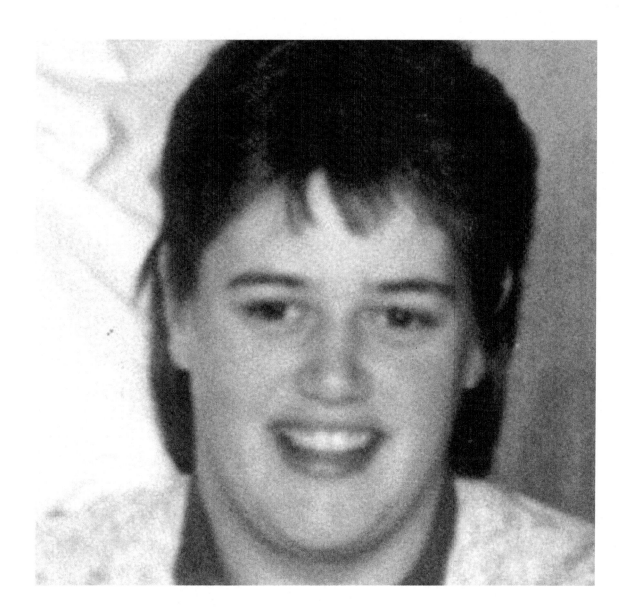

Beverley Allitt is a serial murderer from England who murdered four children and attempted to murder numerous more. Six other people were also seriously injured as a result of her actions. She is regarded as one of England's most renowned serial murderers. She was a nurse who worked at Grantham Hospital in Lincolnshire and was dubbed the "Angel of Death." Though her motivations remain unknown, it has been suggested that she suffers from Munchausen's syndrome via proxy. This mental illness can lead to the urge to murder or inflict harm to others to seek attention. She perpetrated her acts in the hospital's children's ward, where she worked for 59 days between February and April 1991. Her trial judge suggested that she be sentenced to at least 40 years in prison; she was finally sentenced to 30 years. She is presently completing her term at Nottinghamshire's Rampton Secure Hospital. Charlie Brooks played her part in the BBC dramatization of her narrative, titled 'The Angel of Death.'

Childhood and Adolescence

Beverley Gail Allitt was born in Grantham, Lincolnshire, on October 4, 1968. She was raised in the hamlet of Corby Glen. Her mother worked as a school cleaner, while her father, Richard, ran an off-license booze store. Her family consists of one brother and two sisters.

Despite not having any severe injuries, she was known to wear bandages and casts in her early years to attract people's attention. She would also go to hospitals for ailments she didn't have. As a result, her appendix was removed unnecessarily.

She became an outcast as she got older. She allegedly assaulted her partner and made false accusations of rape and pregnancy. Her partner afterward accused her of being pushy, dishonest, and manipulative.

She was accepted into a six-month program at Grantham and Kesteven Hospital in 1991 because they needed additional staff.

She used to do strange things like human smear excreta on the nursing home walls where she studied. She was also absent for the majority of the lessons owing to sickness claims.

Despite her low attendance and examination failures, she was hired on a six-month contract since the hospital was understaffed at the time. She started in the children's ward, where there were two nurses during the day but just one at night. This allowed her misdeeds to go unnoticed for a while.

Crimes

Beverley Allitt began perpetrating her crimes while working at Grantham Hospital. The first victim she abducted was a seven-week-old newborn called Liam Taylor, brought to the hospital with a chest illness. He died on February 21, 1991, and no one suspected foul play.

Timothy Hardwick, an eleven-year-old child with cerebral palsy, was her second victim. After experiencing an epileptic seizure, he was hospitalized. On March 5, 1991, she murdered him.

Becky Philips, her third murder victim, was just two months old and taken to the hospital for gastroenteritis. Claire Peck, a fifteen-month-old girl, hospitalized after having an asthma episode, was her fourth victim. When she was left alone with Allitt, she suffered two heart arrests and died.

Kayley Desmond, Paul Crampton, Yik Hung Chan, Katie Philips, and Bradley Gibson were among the other children Allitt attempted to murder. Fortunately, all five lived and healed after being moved to a different hospital, albeit Katie sustained lifelong brain damage.

The medical personnel only grew suspicious of Claire Peck after her death when it was discovered that she was the sole nurse on duty for all of the children who died or faced significant threats to their lives at the hospital.

Conviction & Trial

Beverly Allitt was finally charged with four charges of murder, eleven counts of attempted murder, and eleven counts of serious bodily harm. She pleaded not guilty to all counts. She was finally found guilty on all counts and sentenced to thirteen concurrent life sentences in prison. She is presently incarcerated in Nottinghamshire's Rampton Secure Hospital.

Her trial judge suggested that she serve a minimum of 40 years in prison and be freed only if she is no longer a threat to society. This was also one of the most severe punishments ever imposed on a woman. She filed an appeal against the length of her sentence, and the High Court decided in December 2007 that she would serve at least 30 years in jail.

She was named as one of the offenders who were ineligible for parole because of her heinous deeds. Because of her activities, the hospital was also forced to close. She is still regarded as one of the most heinous serial killers in English history.

Motives

Though her motivations are unknown, it has been suggested that she has a mental illness known as Munchausen syndrome via proxy. People suffering from the illness are more prone to damage others in their care to draw attention to themselves.

In 2005, the BBC produced a dramatization of her story titled 'Angel of Death.' Her story was also told in an episode of the crime documentary 'Crimes That Shook Britain.'

She appeared in the Netflix series 'Nurses Who Kill' and the series 'Evil Up Close-The Ward Assassin.

8. Peter Manuel

Peter Manuel is Scotland's most notorious serial killer, a brutal psychopath who claimed at least eight victims (and possibly as many as 18) in an orgy of violence between 1956 and 1958. A habitual criminal from the age of 11, Manuel graduated from burglary to rape to murder, killing male and female, young and old, with equal alacrity. "You can have various aspects to a psychopathic personality," Dr. Richard Goldberg of Aberdeen University said in discussing this case. "What is fascinating about Manuel is that he ticks every box."

Manuel was born in New York City on March 13, 1927, the second of three children. His parents Samuel and Bridget, had immigrated to America in the 1920s. But his father's ill health had forced them to return to Scotland in 1932. On their return, they settled briefly in Motherwell before moving south of the border to Coventry.

Manuel struggled to fit in at school and was in trouble from an early age. In 1938, aged just 11, he broke into a chapel and stole money from the collection box. Later that same year, he was caught burglarizing a shop and a house. Those offenses landed him in a reform school, but he habitually escaped to commit burglaries in the area. On October 10, 1941, he broke into a house and threatened the householder with an ax. A year later, during yet another break-in, he struck a woman on the head while she slept, causing concussion and hemorrhage. The woman was hospitalized for some time, while Manuel simply shrugged his shoulders and pled guilty.

By now, the education system was at a loss as to what to do with Manuel. At age 15, he was already a habitual criminal, and no amount of punishment seemed to affect him. His next offense was more serious than breaking. He was charged with indecently assaulting the wife of one of the school staff. After hitting the woman on the head with a stick of wood, Manuel dragged her into some trees, where he ripped off her clothes and tried to rape her. She was found later in a semi-conscious state. She'd suffered a concussion and required eight stitches to her head. Her nose and collarbone had also been broken in the attack.

Manuel again pled guilty. He was also charged with housebreaking and malicious damage to property after discovering that he'd burgled a house and destroyed bedding and clothing by cutting. He'd also scattered foodstuffs and cigarette butts around the scene, something that would become a trademark of his future crimes.

On June 25, 1946, he was sentenced to eight years in Peterhead Prison for the rape. While incarcerated in Peterhead, Manuel expressed his disgust at the way the courts had treated him. He asked to be supplied with various law books and spent much of his time reading up on the Scottish legal system.

But Manuel didn't spend all of his time reading. He was a persistent troublemaker described by prison officers as a 'very unpleasant type of prisoner.' After an incident in 1950 in which he smashed 30 windowpanes and threatened two officers with glass shards, he was examined by a psychiatrist who concluded that he was an 'aggressive psychopath.' The doctor went on to add: "It is doubtful whether, even at the beginning of his sentence, any construction work could have been done with him."

Nonetheless, Manuel was released from his sentence a year early and returned to the family home in Birkenshaw, Lanarkshire. For a while, it looked as though he was trying to go straight. He found a job as a laborer with the Scottish Gas Board and, in the autumn of 1954, started dating a girl named Anne O'Hara, a conductress on the bus he took to work. The following year the couple got engaged, but the relationship floundered and eventually ended over Manuel's refusal to attend church.

Shortly after Anne called off the engagement, Manuel was in trouble again for indecent assault. He defended himself at trial and was acquitted. Not long after, he graduated to murder.

On the afternoon of January 4, 1956, 17-year-old Anne Kneilands was found in woodland adjacent to a golf course at East Kilbride. She'd been brutally battered about the head and evidence suggested that she'd been chased for some distance before her killer had eventually caught up with her and bludgeoned her to death. Although she hadn't been raped, semen stains on her clothing suggested that her killer had masturbated over her corpse.

As they initiated their inquiries, the police learned that a team of Scottish Gas Board employees had been working in the area over the last few days and that one of them had scratch marks on his face. That man was Peter Manuel, already known to officers as a violent offender. Manuel was questioned, and items of his clothing were taken away for forensic examination. He denied any knowledge of the crime, claiming he'd gotten the scratches in a bar fight and had been at home on the night of the murder. Manuel's father corroborated his alibi, and when the tests on his clothes came back negative, the police began focusing their attention on other suspects. However, one officer, Chief Inspector William Muncie, continued to regard Manuel as the man most likely to have killed Anne Kneilands.

Two months after the Kneilands murder, the police got a tip-off that a robbery would take place at a colliery in Blantyre. Manuel was named as one of the two men involved. A trap was laid, and although Manuel managed to escape, he left incriminating evidence at the scene and was soon under arrest.

He was arraigned at Hamilton Sheriff's Court, where he was granted bail. While Manuel was awaiting trial, the police were called to the scene of two burglaries, both bearing Manuel's unique signature - food and cigarette butts scattered across the scene.

Then on the morning of September 17, officers were called to a bungalow in Fennsbank Avenue, High Burnside, close to the scene of the two earlier break-ins. Inside they found the bodies of Marion Watt, 45, her 16-year-old daughter Vivienne and Margaret Brown, Mrs. Watt's sister. All three had been shot dead at close range.

There was spilled food and discarded cigarette butts at the scene, leading police to suspect Manuel immediately. Detectives were dispatched to his home with a search warrant, but they turned up nothing incriminating. Manual also refused to answer any of their questions, and the officers left frustrated.

There'd soon be a new suspect anyway, Mrs. Watt's husband William. He'd been away on a fishing trip in Argyll at the time of the murders, but the investigators suspected he had driven home from the hotel where he was staying, committed the murders, and then returned to continue his holiday. There were plenty of flaws in the theory, but on September 27, Watt was arrested and charged with the murders of his wife, daughter, and sister-in-law. He would be held at Barlinnie Prison for 67 days before being released when detectives eventually admitted they had the wrong man.

Also incarcerated at Barlinnie during that time was Peter Manuel, just starting an 18-month sentence for the attempted robbery at the Blantyre Colliery. Manuel seemed very interested in the Watt case, even asking William Watt's solicitor for a meeting at which he claimed to know the identity of the killer. He refused to give a name, but it was soon obvious that Manuel knew more than he should about the murders. The solicitor passed his suspicions on to the police, but they now believed Manuel was their man; they had no hard evidence against him.

Manuel was released from Barlinnie in November 1957. Within days of his release, he moved to Newcastle-upon-Tyne, ostensibly to find work. On December 8, 1957, a 36-year-old taxi driver named

Sydney Dunn was found dead in his cab on a lonely stretch of moorland in Northumberland. He'd been shot at close range, and his throat had been slit. Manuel had been in Newcastle at the time of Dunn's death but had returned to Scotland when the body was found. Some doubt exists as to whether or not Manuel killed Dunn. He never confessed to the murder. However, two weeks after Manuel's execution, it was revealed that a button matching one of his coats was found in Dunn's cab.

On December 29, 1957, the police received a report that 17-year-old Isabelle Cooke from Mount Vernon had disappeared. The teenager had left home the previous evening to attend a dance and was supposed to meet up with her boyfriend at a bus stop near her Glasgow home. She never arrived. The police mounted a hunt for Isabelle and found various items of her clothing. However, there was no trace of the missing girl.

A week later, the police were called to the scene of another triple homicide. The bodies of Peter Smart, his wife Doris, and the couple's 10-year-old son Michael were found in their home in Uddingston. All three victims were still in their beds. They'd been shot in the head at point-blank range, apparently while they slept.

The police were certain that Peter Manuel was responsible. Proving it, though, was another matter. Manuel had no motive and no links to the victims. No one had seen him enter the home, and very little evidence was left at the scene. They decided to place Manuel under surveillance and detailed a twenty-man team to keep a watch on him. The surveillance team soon hit pay dirt. They noticed that even though Manuel was unemployed, he was spending a lot of time drinking in Glasgow's bars, paying with crisp new banknotes. Following up on this clue, they obtained a few of these notes and took them to Peter Smart's bank. There they learned that Smart had recently made a large withdrawal to pay for a family holiday and that the banknotes Manuel was using could be positively linked to that withdrawal. Finally, they had the evidence they needed.

Early on the morning of January 14, 1958, a little over two years since the murder of Anne Kneilands, Lanarkshire police finally moved in to arrest Peter Manuel. The raid on the family home in Birkenshaw turned up additional evidence - a Kodak camera and a pair of gloves that Manuel had given to his sister and father as Christmas gifts proved to be from one of Manuel's earlier break-ins. Manuel was arrested for housebreaking, his father for receiving stolen goods.

This was a deliberate ploy on the part of the investigation team. They knew that Manuel was very close to his family and that he would not want his father to get into trouble for something he had done. After leaving him alone in his cell for 24 hours, Manuel finally cracked. He offered detectives a deal - drop all charges against his father, and he'd help them 'resolve' certain unsolved cases.

The cops ultimately consented, and Manuel began speaking in front of his parents, admitting in detail to the killings of Anne Kneilands, Marion and Vivienne Watts, Margaret Brown, and the Smart family. He also shocked authorities by admitting to killing Isabelle Cooke. That homicide had not yet been linked to him. Manuel then took authorities to the cultivated area where Isabelle's corpse had been hidden. When authorities inquired about the location of the corpse, he allegedly stated, "I guess I am standing on her."

Manuel was on trial for murder at Glasgow's High Court on May 12, 1958. The trial created quite a stir, with people queuing around the block for a place in the public gallery. They were not disappointed when Manuel fired his counsel and decided to handle his own defense if they were expecting a show. All of those years behind prison studying Scottish law paid off when he filed a request to suppress his admissions, alleging they were delivered under duress. Unfortunately for Manuel, his petition was denied by the judge. The admissions stood, and they helped to create a solid case against Manuel, coupled with evidence regarding the cash stolen from the Smart house and a letter addressed to William Watt's counsel. The jury deliberated for about two hours and 21 minutes before finding him guilty on all charges save the murder of Anne Kneilands (the judge had ruled that the jury should not find Manuel guilty in her case due to lack of evidence).

Manuel was sentenced to death by hanging and was sent to Barlinnie to await his execution. Initially cheery and talkative with the guards, his mental state worsened in the days running up to his death. He refused to talk and ate very little, even rejecting meals for four days at one point. He was often discovered laying on his cot, limbs jerking and foam pouring from his lips. He acquired a shuffling stride with awkward and ungainly bodily motions. In other instances, he'd sigh and whimper on his cot.

The Appeals Court in Edinburgh dismissed his final appeal on June 24. He was sent to Barlinnie, where he continued his farce, no likely in the hopes of convincing the authorities that he was mad. Then, the day before his execution, on July 10, he suffered another change. Manuel, the chatty, upbeat character, had returned.

Manuel met with the prison governor for two hours after a final meal of fish, chips, lettuce, and tomatoes, during which time he is claimed to have confessed to up to 18 unsolved killings. His older brother David paid him a visit at about 8 p.m. Manuel remained awake for the majority of the night after David had departed. He heard Mass and received Holy Communion at 6.50 a.m. At 7:58 p.m., the jail governor and executioner entered the cell. Manuel spoke a few words with the governor, thanking him and his team. Then, turning to the hangman, he said, "Turn on the radio, and I'll go gently." A minute later, he was led across the gallery to the hanging shed, where he was killed at precisely 8 a.m. Manuel was laid to rest in the prison cemetery. At the time of his death, he was 31 years old.

9. Amelia Dyer

Amelia Dyer is regarded as one of history's most heinous and infamous serial murderers. During the Victorian era in England, she is alleged to have murdered approximately 300 newborns whom she had taken in to 'look after.' She was a qualified nurse who engaged in 'baby farming,' a widespread practice in which she cared for unwanted children in return for money. While she conducted her work legally for the first several years, her husband's death threw her off balance. She was convicted and sentenced to six months in jail when children in her care began to die. She began murdering additional children who were placed in her care when she was freed from prison. Throughout her life, she has been admitted to various asylums. Her activities were finally revealed when she was arrested in April 1896. She was hung to death under English law after being accused of various horrific crimes. She has subsequently served as an inspiration for a number of films, novels, and plays.

Childhood and Adolescence

Amelia Dyer was born Amelia Elizabeth Hobley in Bristol, England, in 1836. Samuel Hobley, her father, was a shoemaker, and Sarah Hobley, her mother, was a housewife. The family was not the wealthiest in Pyle Marsh, but they made a good living because of her father's well-established reputation as a skilled shoemaker, which extended beyond the village's borders.

According to records, she grew raised in a large household with four elder siblings. The family led a routine existence, with all of the children attending reputable schools. Amelia excelled in academics and had a strong interest in reading. She used to write a lot of poetry and short tales as a youngster, which pleased her instructors at school.

Typhus hurt her mother's mental health. This quickly became the primary source of anxiety for the entire family. As the fever spread to her brain, she became increasingly aggressive, and the children began to be beaten practically every day as a result. Historians believe that this instilled great hate in Amelia's subconscious mind, which remained suppressed within her.

She gradually began to sink into despair, which was exacerbated by the deaths of two of her sisters. Following her mother's death, Amelia moved to Bristol and lived with her aunt for a time. This assisted her in coming to terms with her mother's passing. She began an internship with a corset manufacturer and studied the technique in the hopes of making a career out of it.

Following her father's death in 1859, her elder brother James fully took over the booming family business. She moved into a Bristol lodge permanently following a disagreement with her brother. She met a man called George Thomas there and married him at the age of 24.

According to some historians, her husband, who was well over 50 years old and a widower, lied about his age in the paperwork and had a few years added to Amelia's age. He is believed to have done this to close the age difference, although there is no evidence to back up this claim.

Her spouse assisted her in enrolling in a nursing school to train as a nurse. Amelia appeared to be content, and she went on to become a successful business in the local "baby farming" sector.

Illegitimate pregnancies were severely stigmatized at the time, and their families did not welcome infants born from such births. Mothers of such newborns were frequently forced to elope with or without their boyfriends, risking exclusion from their families and society.

This increased the activity known as "baby farming." As a result, numerous enterprises engaged in caring such illegitimate newborns in exchange for a fee.

Amelia's nursing background enabled her to make a decent living from her profession.

She put up signs, met with prospective customers, and told them that she was a well-trained nurse and a respectable married lady. She looked to be a sophisticated, well-mannered, and well-spoken woman. As a result, a rising number of newborns were placed in her care.

She began accepting weekly payments, but she accepted more newborns than she could handle in her eagerness for more money. This resulted in her plan to get rid of the children, and over time, many youngsters died under her care.

It is unclear whether these were done on purpose. However, it is suspected that she starved the infants to save money. She is accused of injecting the children with toxic substances, which reduced their appetites and resulted in their deaths.

When the number of deaths grew, she was noted by the public and the law. She was eventually convicted of 'negligence' and sentenced to six months in jail.

Murders & Mental Instability

Amelia grew emotionally disturbed and shown suicidal inclinations while in jail. She is believed to have attempted suicide twice when imprisoned and forced to undertake exceedingly difficult physical labor. She remained depressed for a long period after her release from jail and was even admitted to various mental asylums due to her deteriorating mental condition.

She soon returned to her damaging 'baby farming' techniques, but this time she was more cautious due to the suspicions about her actions that arose after she stay in prison. She relocated frequently.

However, a lot had changed by this point. For example, she was now consciously preparing to dispose of the corpses of the children. She handled everything gently, even hiring a young woman called Jane Smith to assist her. Amelia was very cautious not to tell Jane about her activities and seemed to be a loving mother figure' to avoid suspicion.

She strangled the babies in her care to death with white tapes and then tossed their bodies into the Thames. Doctors couldn't determine if the babies were stillborn or killed at the time. This resulted in no significant action being taken against her, and the number of deceased children increased by the day. The local police department launched an inquiry, but it was incomplete because there were no strong evidence against anybody.

Because she had previously been arrested, Amelia adopted many names to remain unknown. Years of severe alcohol drinking had further altered her face, making it impossible to identify her.

This went on for more than two decades, and the total number of dead bodies surpassed 300. The rising number of demonstrations compelled the police to conduct a thorough investigation. This prompted them to conduct a thorough investigation into the remains discovered in the river.

In 1896, the police got a tip from a tape with an address scrawled on it. Amelia was apprehended soon when the cops tracked her down using the address.

Hanging & Trial

Amelia confessed to her crimes while in police custody, telling officers that they could identify her victims by the "tape around their necks." The court found her guilty in less than six minutes and condemned her to death by hanging.

She attempted to save herself during the trial by claiming that she was mad, but the authorities ultimately showed that it was all a ruse to avoid the death penalty. She confessed to all the killings in front of a chaplain three weeks before the punishment was carried out.

On June 10, 1896, she was hanged at 'Newgate Prison.' "I have nothing to say," she said as she walked away. James Billington carried out her punishment at 9 a.m.

Following Death

The precise number of Amelia Dyer's victims was never established. Still, based on the corpses discovered and the statements of the women who hired her, it is estimated that she murdered between 300 and 400 children. Many individuals protested in the aftermath of the tragedy. Adoption restrictions in the nation were soon tightened.

Some believe she is the same person as another famed Victorian serial murderer, Jack the Ripper, because she was alive and active during his period. Jack the Ripper was never apprehended!

By the same Collection:

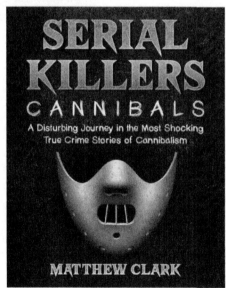

Search on Amazon!!

Printed in Great Britain
by Amazon

21433010R00079